# *Preparation Before The King!*

**Author: Anna Michelle**

Thank you
so much
(Anne Michelle)

ANNA MICHELLE

COPYRIGHT @2015 MICHELLE FRANKLIN

ISBN- 13:978-1535370653 ISBN-10:1535370653

Printed in the United States of America

PUBLISHED BY WRITERS INNOVATION NETWORK (WIN)

This book is available online, and distributors internationally.

This book is dedicated to all my singles that have chosen to do it God's way. No it's not easy, nor does the wait seem to be worth it, but trust it will be. God is not a man that He will lie. If He said He will do it, He will. All you have to do is step aside and let Him. Take your hands off of His plan and watch Him work!

# TABLE OF CONTENTS

# Being Real With Yourself

Throughout most of my life I didn't realize how important building relationships were. Our idea of building relationships is getting people to accept us by trying to make them please us. How can people really please us when most of us don't know enough about ourselves? Due to society we adapt quickly to being who others say is acceptable. *"Every relationship you connect with will be a reflection of how you feel about yourself"*. We all have to start being real with ourselves and others. The reason we need people is because they complete us. Yes! I said they complete us. We are considered whole in Christ. As individuals we need people who have what we don't in order to finish this race. Needing others is a part of our human experience. This is why Jesus didn't start His ministry until He connected with those that were divinely assigned to Him. He wasn't just trying to leave a legacy or be an example of a kingdom leader he needed people.

He was real with them, even those who didn't believe in Him and those who betrayed Him. He didn't become who the systems of this world wanted Him to become. Being real with yourself means you don't expose yourself to everything and everyone. Sometimes exposing too much too soon will cause your vision of you to change. Other peoples view of us matters to us more than we think. TV, radio, church, school, jobs, friends, and family all shape us into who we are. *"Being real with yourself means you must speak up and tell people who you are"*. Never let others define you by your flaws or mistakes, and learn to stand up for yourself. It's time to be real with you and others. Everyone wants to be a leader. But I've learned that being an effective leader means knowing how to build relationships effectively. How can you lead your family if you can't be real with others about your expectations? You don't have to expose everything. People will join you when they can relate to you. This involves…

- *Being passionate about yourself, your vision, and others.*
- *Having compassion for others.*
- *Being open and upfront with what you want and don't want.*
- *Learning your flaws and working on them.*
- *Encouraging yourself and others around you.*
- *Reading the book of Psalms.*
- *Not being afraid of others knowing that you have flaws.*
- *Not being ashamed to reach out for help.*
- *Embracing the idea of transformation.*
- *Being careful who you expose your weaknesses to.*
- *Knowing when it's time to release the real you.*
- *Having faith in God, yourself, and others.*
- *Trusting! If you can't trust yourself, you won't trust others, and they won't trust you.*
- *Being careful who you allow to advise you.*
- *Investing in your personal development daily.*
- *Learning the power of praying.*

When you embrace being real to yourself and others you will become better in your weaknesses and better in choosing the right team/friends or mate.

## Never Assume!

The biggest mistake most people make is when they build relationships based on assumptions. When we see people we usually see them based on flaw lenses. Our perception of others is based on self-freedom. Are you free enough to trust others to be a part of your circle? If not, everyone you meet will be based on your personal imperfections. Jesus recruited followers based on where He was going. He needed people who were divinely ordained because he was leaving a legacy. A legacy that was built on trust. He trusted that in time they would discern the truth about him. The more they followed the more they experienced the truth. In relationships, we must be willing to build. When we break down the word "relationship" it's quite interesting. The word relates means relating to others, having things in common and understanding one another. A ship is a big boat used to transport things. It sails and takes time to get to its destination. So let's define the relationship.

*Relate*- understanding others. *Ship*- takes time to arrive.

If you want to establish a relationship, understanding each other will take time!

You should never assume that everyone is like you or think like you. If you enter into a relationship without putting time restrictions upon it, you will arrive at your destination a lot sooner. Enter in accepting each other. Now I'm not saying accept foolishness. I'm saying be like Jesus and put people in their rightful place in your life. Jesus didn't allow Himself to be transparent in front of all the disciples. He knew who would betray Him and He knew those who would leave. He didn't allow people's assumptions or opinions stop Him from empowering even His enemy. Things to keep in mind.

- *Never assume to know someone, ask questions.*
- *Never assume you are better.*
- *Never assume others can't help.*
- *Never assume what others have said about you are true.*
- *Never rely on your perception of others when building relationships.*
- *Never assume others flow like you.*
- *Never assume that my behavior at that moment defines my character.*

- *Never assume others lack the capacity of trust. We all can be trustworthy.*

- *Never assume that the world revolves around you.*

- *Never assume based on appearance.*

Remember your assumption is an enemy when it comes to building relationships. It will limit you from advancing, because you can't advance without the help of others. When you assume, it's a reflection of a carnal mind that has become self-centered. We are never supposed to wrongly judge people. Judging is the main issue in our churches and nations today. The only way to be effective in leading is through relationships which are created through influence, and you can only influence through your character. Being real with yourself and others will help you in your singleness, so when God sends your mate you will be ready to build!

# Introduction

I believe there are a lot of singles that have a false image of what it means to be a godly wife. Every woman in the body of Christ has a different process. However, in today's society some women are being told to be prepared for failure. I've been to many conferences where we were told that God is not going to send us a spouse if we didn't own something, have a degree, or simply put have our own everything. As I lay before the Lord seeking answers, waiting for the manifestation of my spouse I realize all God requires is for us to be disciplined, committed, open, and good stewards over what He has given us. I believe that once the foundation of Christ has been laid, God will begin to build us into the person our spouse is going to need. I am not saying that we shouldn't take ownership of our lives and produce in our singleness, but God Is a builder and He's not building according to our past or present but according to our future. We need to be able to accommodate each other where we are going. If you are looking for your spouse, God is not looking for self-center carnal individuals. He's looking for someone who understands the value of a partnership, and someone who depends on Him. God wants to accommodate and secure your future. When He sends your mate, he or she will be able to carry you in the future. Now let's define accommodate.

*Accommodate*- to provide lodging or sufficient space. To hold and make adjustments to suit a particular purpose. It involves making changes to fit someone's needs, and your ability to come in agreement with each other.

The bible says how can two walk together except they agree? God wants us to accommodate each other because He wants you to be in agreement with each other. When you lack the capacity to accommodate each other you won't be able to satisfy one another's future. Its during our singleness where God makes the necessary changes we need in order to adjust to our mate. Our tests are designed to make us stronger so we can stand and fight for each other. We must be able to accommodate each other's present and future desires and our God-given assignments. *"When we accommodate someone's future, it means we make a commitment to grow for the good of our relationship"*. When you don't allow God to shape your mate you will connect to the wrong one and lose yourself. Throughout the years, I've heard people say that somewhere along the way they lost themselves because they were trying to satisfy their mate. God builds according to our future, so when you allow Him to choose your mate your future will be secure!

# The Foundation

Growing up I was always taught, if you want a husband to find a friend. Church, family, and society teaches us that the best and long lasting relationships are defined by our ability to befriend each other. How can I find a male friend? It's not easy. Anytime a woman tries to connect with a man with intent to establish a friendship, it usually becomes a mental, physical, and emotional war. As I search for answers from a biblical perspective I realized that there were no scriptures to support dating for a long period of time or even waiting till friendships were established. Which poses a question? What is the foundation for relationships? And how do we lay a solid foundation that will last? Although there're no scriptures to support the friendship before dating theory. The bible teaches us about relationships.

*Building relationships are the foundation of the kingdom!*

It's when we build successful relationships that we are able to learn from each other. There were many times I tried to build a relationship with a man in hopes it will lead to something more; it was something we both agreed on. Well, it almost broke me. A lot of times men want to act like you're dating without making a greater commitment, as do women. There are many types of friends these days, so the question is when you decide to become friends what type of friendship do you have? When I agreed to connect with a person on the basis by being friends first in an effort to establish a relationship, it fails because of the expectations that were placed on it. When you connect as friends with intent to progress, you give the relationship direction. Doing that is what causes an emotional war. It's important that we understand who we are before entering into any relationship. If men and women don't submit to their process they will never have a successful marriage. The process was created to help you understand your purpose and the purpose of your marriage. Marriage was created by God with a purpose. It was God's intention to bring people together (man and woman) in order to build a nation, an empire. How do I become a wife? That was a question I never asked myself until now. I thought that when people meet, have sex, and fall in love that this means marriage is probably going to happen. However, as I learned more about God I realize that God is the only one that can give us the right spouse. If we want a long, full and prosperous life, we have to connect with the vision He has for our lives. Lets look at Genesis.

*Genesis 2:18 and the Lord God said it is not good for man to be alone; I will make him a help meet.*

When God looked upon man He saw a need. Now two things happened here. First, God created someone to assist Him with His assignment (the first mandate). Then God gave them more work and told them to produce an increase. God built someone who would help Him carry out His assignment. The foundation for every marriage is a godly man and woman. When God created Adam He laid the foundation within him first. He had to mold him and shape him into His image. Once God built Adam, He placed him in the garden and gave him an assignment. It is within man's assignment that God noticed that it was not good for man to be alone. For his obedience God wanted to give him an increase by sending someone who would help him produce life. That means when a man and woman come together they are suppose to create life. Not just babies, but they have the ability to bring life to every dead thing in their lives. Hint! Everything is not going to be alive and well when you meet. I believe that there are areas in our lives that will awaken when we link up with our mate.

*Genesis 2:21-25*

*And the Lord God caused a deep sleep to fall upon Adam, and he slept: and he took one of his ribs, and closed up the flesh instead thereof; and the rib, which the Lord God had taken from man, made he a woman and brought her to the man. And Adam said this is now bone of my bones, and flesh of my flesh: she shall be called woman because she was taken out of the man. Therefore, shall a man leave his father and mother and shall cleave unto his wife: and they shall be one flesh. And they were both naked, the man and his wife and were not ashamed.*

Most of the time you hear about a singles conference it's always geared toward single women. We are always told to stay in our process and allow God to send us our spouse. However, when I read this text it explains why a lot of men end up choosing the wrong mate. *Adam was placed in a deep sleep that was his process.* Sleep is a process that the body goes through in order to restore its levels of energy. It is a state of both physical and mental well-being. It gives you rest, helps you relieve stress, and helps you recover from illnesses that have weakened the body from its normal functions. Sleep consists of four stages and is also a natural cycle of activity in the brain which consists of two basic states. Rapid eye movement and not - rapid eye movement. When a person first falls asleep they usually are in stage one. During stage one there is little to no eye movement and one can be wakened without difficulty. Little to no eye movement means that a person may not experience as many dreams and may end up sleep walking. Sleepwalking is very dangerous! When you sleep walk you are not in control of your actions, you are unaware of your surroundings, and will do just about anything that you wouldn't usually do even kill someone. Some researchers say it's like talking to a dead person.

## Stage two

Stage two is known as light sleep in which the heart rate slows and the body temperature decreases. It is at this point that the body begins to move into deep sleep.

## Stages three and four

Stage three and four are the deep sleep stages. If aroused from sleep during these stages a person may feel **confused** and **disoriented**. During stages three and four the body will also repair, regenerate, build bone muscle, and strengthen the immune system. In other words, the body will heal itself. Now, just the fact that God placed him in a deep sleep is awesome. He removed one of his ribs because his body could heal and regenerate itself. When a men has gone as far as they could go (without his help meet), God will place them in a deep sleep process in order to build the woman they will need. I believe that during the deep sleep process the man wakes up too soon confused and disoriented, (not in his right mind). When that happens he begins to choose a wife based on the foundation that has been laid. *Just because she is a godly woman doesn't mean she's your wife.* Your wife needs to be built for you and your assignment. When God lays the foundation, it's only the beginning of getting to know Him, (God). When we become rooted in Christ He reveals and shapes us to fulfill our purpose, and our mate has to fit into that purpose. Eve was a part of Adam's purpose in the garden and for the earth. God added to the assignment Adam already had. When He formed Eve she had to be able to accommodate him in his ministry.

**Genesis 1:29 says that God gave them every herb that yields seed on the earth and every seed that yields seed for food.**

That's a full-time business. He gave them ownership and dominion over everything on the earth. What God gave them was a partnership. I use to ask God why He couldn't just send me a man who loves me and who will be good to me. I know it's some out here, those were my thoughts. After years of praying, I now realize why God hid me. He was preserving me for my king. In December of 2010 I was told that it was my season for marriage. I was excited! But when I didn't see the manifestation of it I was upset with God. I didn't want to hear anything about the prophetic ever again. Don't prophesy to me, and don't touch me! But then God used a friend to convince me to go away to a conference she was attending in Green Bay, Wisconsin. It was there that God began to restore my passion for believing again. He told me that there is seed time and harvest time. Seed time is where he begins to prepare us for our spouse. He reminded me of the partnership I had entered into with a friend. The next morning I heard Him whisper in my ear. *The footsteps of the righteous are ordered by the Lord (Psalms 37:23).* As I sat up He said I can't send you a spouse until you understand the true value of a partnership. He said to me, you need to maximize this season and start learning for the partnership you are in. The next day I started to write this book.

### Seed time

During our seed time God is testing what my spiritual leader (Apostle Benny L. Dozier) calls our weight carrying capacity. He's looking for godly principles, and to see if our hearts have been penetrated with the fruits of the spirit. These are all the things we are taught in the beginning stage. This is why laying the foundation is important. Before Esther was able to marry the king she had to go through her season of preparation. When God hears our spouse heart He will send us. We don't have to worry and we don't have to live up to other people's standards.

*Proverbs 18:22 He who finds a wife finds a good thing, and obtains favor from the lord.*

Find means to discover after full consideration. Also, to regain the use of, recover, or relocate something that has been lost. You are now in search of something that has been taken away from you. Now let's try again. He who relocates what has been taken away from him recovers a good thing and obtains favor from the Lord. When God took Adam's rib and created Eve, God was simply giving him what had been taken away from him. So if I can encourage the men to do anything it would be to wait, seek the Lord. Stop trying to find a wife who will live up to your standards and not God. Stay in your process because it is within the process you will find that God is building your perfect mate. Don't settle for what has been laid. Allow God to build the person that can handle your future. Man may not be perfect, but everything God does will always be perfect!!!

## *Q&A*

Has the foundation been laid within you?

Do you understand your purpose?

Are you in seed time or harvest time?

Are you ready to be found?

Note taking below!

## *Building In His Image*

After the foundation of Christ has been laid, God can now start to build. In this process, God begins to build your character. Let's look at the process it would take to build a house. When you are building a house it is very important to have regular inspections to make sure the structure and the foundation is strong. The house must be able to stand against storms, cold weather, or even something as simple as people walking around. It must be stable; if the house is not inspected periodically during the construction process you can miss something and may be required to go back and uncover any work that wasn't inspected. Why are inspections done? Inspections are done to catch any potential problems before construction is finish. A house can be built on sand but will likely fall after a short period because your not building on the right foundation *(Matthew 7:26)*.

Having a house built from the ground up is one of my dreams. Its takes a lot of thought, because this is going to be a place where I live, maybe the rest of my life. Although I've had plans to have a house built I never thought about the foundation. That's usually something that you don't think about until you move and start feeling the earthquakes. Again the foundation must be stable if your new house is going to be able to stand. Positioning is very important. If you began to build a house on a huge piece of land, you could make a mistake by claiming part of someone else land thus causing a setback in your building process. Three years ago I wanted to buy a house. I begin to seek out advice from people and I didn't like their responses. I was asked one question. Have you counted up the cost? I was mad. I thought I was ready because I had been paying rent since I was eighteen years old. But what I learned was that a house has a lot more expenses than renting an apartment. Do you have enough stored up in case something breaks down and are you discipline enough to cut back? That's why it is imperative that you stay within the guide lines of what you can afford. Everyone may not be prepared to carry the responsibility.

*Luke 6:47*

*Why do you call me Lord and do not the things I say. Whoever comes to me and hearth my saying and doth them I will show you to whom he is like. He is a man who builds a house, and dug deep, and laid the foundation on a rock: and when the flood arose the stream beat vehemently upon that house and could not shake it, for it was founded upon a rock. But he that heareth and doeth not are like a man that without a foundation built a house upon the earth against which the stream did beat vehemently and immediately it fall and the ruin of that house was great.*

Building a house is not much different than God's process of building us. God first lays the foundation of Christ in our lives so that everything else will be able to stand. The only reason we are stable is that He has taken up residency on the inside of us. How will any relationship be able to stand against adversity if we as individuals are not stable? God has to mold us back into His image by building our character. He wants us to be men and women of integrity. He wants to renew our minds, and allow His word to penetrate through the walls of our heart. From the beginning, God had plans for us. He carefully thought out every detail of our lives. Just like building a house takes planning God plans. He does regular inspections of our lives. He told Jeremiah that He knew him before he was in the womb He called and ordained him to be a prophet unto the nations. In essence what God was saying is that His thoughts manifest into the womb of women. So when God builds us for our spouse He plans, He strategizes every detail of our assignment and our future. You and your spouse have an assignment. When we understand the value of a partnership that is when we will be ready for our spouse. Everyone goes through some form of training. Adam learned the true meaning of a partnership in the garden. Every animal had someone who was comparable to its kind, and we all know how protective animals are over each other. It was in watching them that I believe he learned partnership. About five years ago I met this lady who told me that her husband was diagnosed with prostate cancer. After everything she had been through in her life she stated that she wasn't equipped for that. She couldn't help him. All she talked about was herself and her needs. That's when I looked up to the sky and went off on our daddy God.

I don't have anyone but yet you allow someone like this to. I was at a loss for words. But now I understand that even though the vows say for better or for the worst we still need to be built for our mates. As I stated before we need to be able to accommodate each other where we are going. God knows that the enemy will try and attack our bodies, so He will build someone who can deal with those kinds of sicknesses. In the building process, you want to watch out for decoys *(imitations of your spouse)*. I know a lot about this. When I was told it was my season of marriage God told me to watch out because the enemy was getting ready to send a decoy. He did. There were so many men coming at me I asked the Lord to rebuke them. Don't get me wrong I loved the attention, however, I ran into someone who caused my flesh to be woken up. Needless to say, I ran. Another thing I want to address concerning the building process is positioning. Please don't try to covet someone else's mate. If you do you might run into a headache.

Over the years, I've heard a lot of women praying for someone else's man. They say things like Lord if my spouse is with someone else break them up and send them to me. The question is are they ready for you? If God spoke to you and told you that he/she is your spouse, then pray and ask God to let His will be done in His time in your lives. Everything is about positioning, being at the right place at the right time. *Let's look at Jacob!*

If Jacob weren't on the run from Esau he wouldn't have been at the right place at the right time to meet Rachel. God is trying to build a nation through your marriage. Jacob married Rachel and together they birth Joseph who was able to empower a nation. When you are single and have embraced your assignment, the enemy gets mad, but when you connect with the person God sends you, the power of God manifest and the enemy is defeated. The devil wants us to develop a false attitude of contentment in an effort to destroy marriages. We are supposed to be content with everything through Him (God). There are many people quoting *Philippians 4:11* where Paul is addressing the Philippians church because of their concern for him. Paul stated that he learned to be content with what he had; he went on to say he can do all things through Christ who strengthens him. What he was saying is that he learned how to be satisfied through Christ. His relationship with Christ gave him the confidence to believe all his needs would be met.

There are a lot of believers that quote that verse and have not allowed the state of satisfaction in Christ to penetrate their hearts, which can only be obtained through the Spirit. So when two people come together, believe that they have chosen the right mate, and they end up in divorce court. *Why?* Because they were never content in their spirit man, Most of the couples I've spoken to say they had no fight in them. Many of them believe that it's easy being single, so they enter into the marriage thinking they could have done with or without it. They are so content in their flesh, that their mindsets are I don't need this man or woman, I'm independent. I thought talking with married women would help me become a great wife one day, until I realized that so many women today didn't wait on God and are struggling for their identity.

I believe God wants us to be content and dependent on Him. Content also means that you have accepted being without something rather than wanting more or better. I have accepted loving Christ and making Him the head of everything in my life. There is no need of wanting more (no one supersedes Christ). But as a single woman I have not accepted being single; I want a husband and the bible says to make your request known to God *(Philippians 4:6)*. You have to believe God will do it, and stop allowing people to tell you to stop praying and just be content with what you have. Nothing is wrong with wanting more as long as it doesn't take the place of Christ in your life.

## *Q&A*

Do you have a strong foundation?

Have you made your request(s) known?

Are you content?

Note taking below!

# Capacity

Capacity refers to the maximum amount that something can be contained and your ability to perform a task. Your capacity is very important when you get married because you must be able to handle each other. First, you must learn what God has said about your capacity. Please understand that capacity is not something you can learn from reading books, but must be attained through experience. God will test your capacity through your trials in an effort to promote you to greater levels. I have come across many women who seem to be very discouraged when they think about the idea of God sending them a husband in their weakest and poorest moments. Again God will test your weight carrying capacity in your singleness. In the times of lack, sickness, and what seems to be hopelessness, can you stand and fight? How much pressure can you handle without throwing in the towel? In the mist of adversity can you stand and build up your prayer life and remain faithful to what God has promised you? How well do you deal with transitioning? And how many assignments will be completed or left incomplete? If your assignment includes children, how well can you multitask as a wife, mother, sister, daughter, counselor, business owner, and as an individual? During that process God may send your spouse. *Why?* Because He's God! And He has His reasons. During our building process God will send people to minister to our needs in our broken state. So why do we find it hard to believe He will send someone a spouse who has not been saved long? The key is knowing your process and what you can handle.

*1 Corinthians 10:13*

**But God is faithful; he will not suffer you to be tempted beyond that which ye are able to bear.**

If there is anything we can't handle, God is not going to release it to us. That's why He takes us through a process to show us if we are ready for the blessing or not. He knows if we are ready, but we need to see. Now Sarah was the wife of Abraham and the mother of Isaac. God chose to change her name to make her a mother of nations. God told Abraham that he and Sarah would bear a son in their old age. Sarah laughed! God knew that even in her old age she would be able to carry the promise, but she needed to see. God enlarged her capacity to build a nation, through her womb. The women in the bible are awesome examples for the women of today. They loved and respected their husbands. They were full of wisdom, patience, and were willing to do anything to be a part of God's plan. All of them had a different capacity and we can learn from their struggles. They knew how important is was to produce children so they kept praying seeking the Lord and did whatever it took to get one. Some women have the capacity to have one child. Not that they can't have them but it's about knowing how many you can handle.

### Matthew 25:15

**And unto one, he gave five talents, to another two, and to another he gave one. To every man he gave according to his ability and straightway took his journey.**

As women, we need to stop being consumed with looks, money, and pulpit fame. Yes, I said it pulpit fame. Most of the time, we seem to want to be connected with men standing behind the pulpit. Don't get me wrong I want a man who is after God's heart. Men who preach and teach the word of God, but at the end of the day can you handle it? Can you take the pressure of being married to a superstar? It's not for everybody. We have to get to a point in our lives when we are willing to take ownership of our inventory. You must be built for that. If you want to be great, your capacity to hold it must be greater. Capacity is not based on what you have but what's on the inside of you. If God has not cleaned you out, you don't know what's on the inside of you. After being in ministries for eleven years, serving in leadership even teaching, I've come to realize that the foundation of Christ had been laid, but I hadn't completed the building process. After eleven years I still saw myself as weak and little, but today I see the enemy for who he really is and that's a thief. He comes to deceive women into thinking they don't need a man to help them carry out the assignment(s) God has given them (when they are in a relationship). God is going to send you what you need, his standards. Another sign that the enemy is deceiving you is when you think God is going to send you someone who has money, cause you got money. Ok, you got money. Being with someone based on their credentials or their Jesus quotes they post on Facebook isn't God. Don't get me wrong we must accomplish some things in life - be good stewards, clean up our credit and buy a piece of land. But don't discredit the person God has for you based on material things. If you do, that's ok because you will end up with someone who is just as carnal as you.

### Romans 8:6-10

**For to be carnally minded is death; but to spiritually minded is life and peace.**

What does it mean to be carnally minded? Simply put having fleshly desires and a natural state of mind. It means you are always concerned about your needs and not God's. God knows what we need and what we are going to need in a relationship. I believe he has different strategies for every marriage to work and experience wealth. Please don't allow the enemy to put you in a box. Sit back and allow God to build you expand you and equip you to flow on whatever level you and your spouse will be on.

## *Q&A*

List the things you can't handle?

Are you willing to take on more responsibility?

How many assignments are left incomplete?

Note taking below!

# Discipline

Upon entering into the world we are trained to do just about everything. From walking, talking, and to even eating three to five meals a day. As we get older we get away from a lot of disciplining that was implemented in our life as a child. In order for us to be discipline, we must be trained to perform daily tasks. As humans, we tend to lose focus on those routines because we get comfortable. Comfortable because someone came along and introduced us to something else. When men and women come into the knowledge of Christ we are required to discipline our minds and bodies to look more like him. It's a process we go through after we are reborn. Just like a natural babe has to be trained to function so does babes in Christ. Discipline is what makes us produce. This is one reason why it is important that we allow God to discipline us. He's trying to get us to produce a good harvest and create stability. *Discipline is the power to control, motivate, and train oneself by way of instruction(s).*

It is likely done in areas that need improvement, and is not a good feeling. As we begin to grow we get use to doing things our way. This is one of the reasons why counseling and courtship before marriages are important. During that time you both will be able to discuss your weaknesses (the areas that need improvements) and set goals. God will also train us to be discipline in our ministry in an effort to train us for our spouse. He wants us to be in partnership with the church (both parties actively helping to bring the vision together).

*Proverbs 25:28*

*A person without self-control is like a house with its doors and windows knocked out.*

When a couple does not have self-control, any and everything will be able to come in and attack the relationship. If you haven't trained your mind to fight the spirit of lust in your singleness you won't win the battle. I say lust because lust is an area we all deal with. Whether its lust for money, cars, or people we all have things that are attached to our flesh that God is going to have to shred at some point in our lives. There are a lot of things I had to shred in my singleness that I didn't understand, like drinking. I know a lot of people that have a glass of wine from time to time. As for me, drinking was something I was told I couldn't do. Do you know the strategies and the standards that God has set for your life?

We all have a different assignment that requires different forms of discipline. When it comes to men and women we are told to have standards. How would you know what your standards are if you don't know what God has said about you personally? Stop going by someone else's process, and life. What discipline produces in your singleness will create stability in your marriage? October of 2013, God woke me up and had me to write a prayer concerning my spouse. I was to say that prayer every day. I said it every day for about four days and stopped. During my morning walk, I heard the Lord say, a wife must intercede for her husband. In my singleness, God was calling me to make a wall of defense for my marriage. As you become discipline praying for your marriage, not only will it just flow in your marriage, but it will help us avoid some things. As I stated before we are used to doing things our way when we have been single for a long period, so don't think you don't need to be trained to be a wife.

The message bible says in *Galatians 5:22 when you are discipline, you will develop a willingness to stick with things*. When God starts calling you for more discipline, he's up to something. He wants to bless you with something you need, want and something He's saying you can now handle. Discipline creates the momentum you need to keep fighting for it. The enemy is going to attack you both, and everything you've learned in your discipline process will prepare you to win the battle. When Jesus came into the world He came into the flesh to show us that the flesh has no power over us. He was trained in His toddler stages, His teen stages, and as an adult. Before He started His ministry He was driven into the wilderness. Even though He was trained in the natural things, He could not start His ministry until He was trained in all things.

### Matthew 17:14 Jesus healed a boy with a deaf and dumb spirit.

The boy's father brought him to the disciples but they could not cast it out. Jesus told them this kind comes out through fasting and praying. In essence, what He was saying was that some things are only going to be produced through discipline. So while we are waiting for our King lets maximize every season and allow God to discipline us in the areas that need improvements. Habits are created through discipline and discipline creates a lasting effect.

## Q&A

What habits are you forming?

Why is discipline important?

What are some of the things discipline can do for you?

Note taking below!

# Commitment

What is the different between a commitment and a covenant relationship? A covenant is a legally binding contract while a commitment is an act of devotion and responsibility to keep your promise to that contract. Whenever I pray and ask God for a spouse all I would say is, I need someone to love me and to be good to me. It was upon me writing this book I realized that good and love are expressions of how we feel and feelings change. So now what? What is going to be the glue that holds my marriage together? One word was spoken, *Commitment!* I pray every day that I and my spouse would be committed not just to each other but that we will be committed to the promise we made before God. Even when we don't feel loved or feel lonely, we will be willing to seek help.

Commitment can be applied to many things. I am committed to keeping my goal of walking every morning for an hour, and staying committed to things I've started. The only way discipline is going to be able to bear fruit is through commitment. Your mind has to be committed to the vision and your heart. You cannot be willing to give up, and must be willing to stand and fight. Committed to something or someone also means you are not seeking for a replacement. You have set the goals connected to the relationship and you're not looking to replace it with anything or anyone else. Staying devoted will bring success and not failure. Failure happens in a lot of relationships because no one is willing to stay committed to one or more things. I have spoken to many women/men who say that their spouse stops being committed to helping out with the kids, the finances, and even church. Yes church! These three things are some of the reasons many are throwing in the towel. Now I don't pretend to know why a lot of marriages end in divorce. Often times I ask myself if it was due to a lack of commitment to the relationship or a lack of commitment servicing each other as partners. As partners, each person has a role in helping to make the vision of the house function. I heard from one lady that she made most of the money and her husband had bad spending habits. I was told by another that her spouse didn't want to help with the kids or household chores. These are some of the things we need to watch out for and be praying about in our singleness. If you know you have a problem with spending, let the other person deal with the finances or seek help. We also have to remind ourselves not to put all the work on one person. (I've been single for 34 years and I wish I would marry somebody who wants me to do all the work). That was a side note. As a mother of two, my children are at an age where they can help with cleaning, washing, and even cooking. As a single parent things would often get a bit overwhelming because everything was my reasonability. It's the same way in marriage. We should never make the other feel overwhelmed with the overall vision. A marriage isn't a marriage without the involvement of two people so everyone should play their part.

So now a ***Covenant is a legally binding contract***. I know many people like to think that all marriages are built on a covenant with God but they're not. Everyone doesn't believe in God. As singles, we must get acquainted with the covenant. You can't commit to the covenant if you don't know or understand it. We often think that saying the vows mean we understand the covenant. Many believe that as long as they love each other that cover the covenant. One of the things I now understand about God's covenant is that it always benefits someone else. So outside of love why are you connected? Many times God will bring two people together to build, restore, and deliver a nation. That's why the enemy is after marriages so hard, he tries to stop them from building this nation under God. He knows that when two people come together on one accord, who understands their purpose, and know who they are in God, then they become a force to be reckoned with. In the beginning, he wasn't concerned about deceiving Adam until God decided to link him up with someone who would help him produce an increase. Even the enemy understood the significance of more than one. When you understand that, things will begin to speed up in your marriage. As singles, it's hard to pay off something when it's just you. Two-paychecks are always better to work with than one. To better understand a partnership let's look closely at the church. Once I was at a point in my life where I felt lost and like the ministry didn't need or appreciate me. I felt lonely from time to time and was at the point of losing my passion for God. When you are in a relationship, it's not just about you giving your time, money, and creativity, but you need to feel like you are receiving from the other as well. I found myself not going to church like I use to (at least to all the functions). Until one day I heard the Lord say.

*"Even when you don't feel needed, loved, or appreciated you must remain committed to the vision"*. I repented right there in the middle of the gym. I began to meditate on what it meant to really be connected or disconnected. So I asked myself if I was really connected to the vision in the first place. For instance, when you plug a cord into the outlet in the wall, we think that it's connected because it fit. But just because it fit don't mean there isn't a shortage. A lot of time we join ministries because they look like they are going somewhere, we like how they make us feel, or because we've heard nice things about them. Well, it's the same way in a relationship. You can't stay connected or reconnect to something you were never connected to in the first place. So while you are in this season of preparation I challenge you to get connected to individuals you are supposed to be connected to. In the end, you will find yourself fighting for what belongs to you. Remember God is a covenant keeper, and He lives on the inside of you. So pray that He will empower you and your spouse to be covenant keepers as well.

## Q&A

Are you connected?

Is there a shortage in your communication between you and your mate?

Are you a covenant keeper?

Note taking below!

# Partnership

A partnership is an arrangement in which both parties agree to cooperate to advance their mutual interests. Whenever two people enter a partnership they usually decide to bring all skills and resources together. It's a joint venture where both parties share in the profits and losses. Let's take a closer look. When you become partners, it's because of attraction. Nothing more nothing less. Either they look good or they have skills, talents, and resources that you believe you need and you also believe that they may be able to help you get an increase. Everyone in the partnership has agreed to take responsibility and ownership of the vision. It means that you have sat down and decided who was going to be the lead and you trust that they are capable of leading. Yes, it's a partnership, but someone has to take the lead in order to establish order. Now it was God intentions for the man to take the lead, that's why he said in *1 Corinthians 11:3* that the head of every woman are man.

Although God made us equals I believe God will pour out the revelation and the vision to the husband. In the book of *Genesis* when Adam and Eve ate of that tree, God approached the man because the man should have known better. Not because God made him first but because he made him the leader of the partnership. Remember John C. Maxwell said everything rises and falls on leadership. When it comes to partnership, I know it all too well. It was something I always wanted to do. I always believed that if I had someone to help me, things would get moving. So I decided to go for it. But without studying, praying, and even searching the web I found myself walking away from a bitter relationship. Every time I looked up I was jumping into it head first. There were no business plans; no structure formed not even a mission. Who's going to contribute what? What Challenges may come up or what is our target markets? At the time, I didn't even trust the individuals. I've been in a partnership three different times. We had no obligations to each other because we both wanted to take the lead and be in control without taking responsibility for it. We didn't view each other as equals and we didn't have a willingness to learn from each other. We weren't willing to accept each other's differences, and we didn't have a desire to exchange our gifts, wisdom, and talents for the overall vision. What can I say the list could go on and on, but I'll stop there? Now I know many would say why go into a partnership? These are the things we should have discussed upon entering into this type of agreement, and it's always good to team up with someone else. Remember two is better than one.

Over the years, I've learned that when two people share similar interests, it doesn't mean that they will make a great team. That's why it's important that we pray about everything. God knows who we need to help us move forward. When you enter a partnership with an individual mindset, it will always be easy to try and control everything. Singles are always being told to own something and make their own money. All that's good but there needs to be a balance and that balance need to be God. I believe that in today's society singles are preparing for failure. We are told to store up just in case the marriage doesn't work, and you won't be left with nothing. It's what I like to call the what if factor. Several years ago God spoke to me about this big hindrance. He begins to show me how basing our lives on what if is fueled by fear. Most of us don't try and buy a house because what if we can't afford the upkeep.

Now I know the bible tells us to write the vision and make it plain. But what does that mean? We have to count up the cost of everything. Start saving and doing a little investing on the market. Simple put start preparing yourself by disciplining your finances and staying committed to the vision. As I stated before, we must produce in our singleness. There were a lot of things Adam could not do for himself. Therefore, God sent someone to help him in the areas he needed help in. I don't know about anyone else but there are some things I need help with. Women tend to think if they are independent they are better off. I know because that was my mindset. I remember telling people that when God sends my husband he's going to have to add on to what I already have. He's not coming in making anything because I'm going to have my own everything. I was wrong and I was taught that way by the women in the church who already had a man. The same women who didn't know how it felt to be without a man when many of them got save and got married it were because it was better to marry than to burn. Then they gone come to try and tell me how to be single (side note). When God sends our spouse all He requires is discipline, and for us to have a willing heart, committed to serving Him, and be men and women of integrity. Anything else is extra and a plus! In our season of transformation, God will open up doors for us to get wealth in our singleness, but it will not be the reason He sends our spouse.

God wants us to be depended on Him not money, not things, and certainly not a spouse. By the time I enter the third partnership, I realized God was setting me up for marriage. When I talked to my leader about going into business with another member of the church, he told me to let her lead because she had more business experience. I said yes. I was ready and because I had a desire to change my current situation this gave me the momentum I needed to submit to someone else. Although we shared similar interests of the business it was really hard to stay connected. We both wanted to own a thrift store. However, each of us had different plans on how we wanted it to advance. The first mistake was not sitting down and discussing a plan and structure of the business. We were excited, and because of the Lord, I was able to see why He allowed me to partner with her at that time. I needed to listen and not move out when I get an idea. I am very creative and ideas just flow at any given time. So God needed to place someone in my life who would tell me slow down sister you doing too much. We had a mutual understanding and we grew to trust each other. God's reason for the link up was to increase us and I appreciated it. I increased in wisdom, business, and another level of submission. An excellent example of a partnership was Aquila and Priscilla. They were both tent-makers working in the marketplace. They worked together, were equals, and had no room for jealousy. Can you imagine the Apostle Paul needing a place to stay, God sending him there, and the husband goes into a jealous rage? Another thing partners must be able to do is receive from each other.

I'm not just talking about gifts. Everyone in the relationship has something to add to it, so don't ever think that you are carrying the relationship. The responsibility belongs to you both which means you are carrying each other. The number one spirit that seems to be released on relationships is the spirit of pride. When one person is contributing a little bit more they start saying things like we wouldn't be where we are if it wasn't for them. When you think like that it sometimes become hard to receive wisdom or revelation from each other. If you can't receive from each other, then you can't connect and receive a harvest. Remember when two people come together it's because they have something in common. Their hopes and dreams are usually alike and they believe they can help bring an increase to each other.

## Q&A

Are you ready to partner up?

Why is having a partnership good?

Partners must be willing to submit to each other. Are you ready to submit?

Note taking below!

# Producing Our Harvest

Once you have become disciplined and committed to the partnership then you will be able to produce a harvest. When God brought Adam and Eve together, he told them to be fruitful, multiply, and to replenish the earth *(Genesis 1:28)* tells us that God planted a field on the earth, but no herb had grown because the Lord had not caused it to rain on the earth, for there was no one to till the ground. God has a plan to prosper every couple. He said He planted a field that had no herbs because no one was available to take care of it. An herb symbolizes wealth, and even though God gave you and your spouse the idea to start that business He will not rain on your seed if you are not prepared to bring an increase. As I stated before we are supposed to produce in our singleness and an even greater increase in our marriage. Whenever God gives us an assignment it has the ability to keep producing a harvest. All he needs is for us to make the connection with discipline and commitment. He wants us to live a full and prosperous life as singles and as husbands and wives.

One reason why it's important to know what your assignment is in your singleness is    everything that was manifested in your singleness is supposed to enlarge us when we link up with our spouse. God will blow on everything and cause it to increase. In the beginning, God was providing for the vision he had given Adam and Eve. Now let's discuss the fruits of the spirit. I believe that these fruits will be the glue that keeps your relationship growing. Again commitment and discipline will produce these gifts.

*But the fruit of the spirit is love, joy, peace, long-suffering, gentleness, goodness, faith, meekness, temperance, against such there is no law.*

To be *long-suffering* you must be patience with each other. Sometimes we want what we want when we want it, but is it time to have it? Long-suffering is only manifested when you trust each other. IF you can exercise patience before the relationship, you will have it in the relationship. *Meekness* means to be humble. The only way to be submissive in a partnership is to allow the Lord to humble you. Your idea doesn't always have to be used. Remember you don't always have the best answer, and you must value each other so you can produce a greater harvest. *Faith* means to have confidence and trust in someone other than you. Simply put you don't mind allowing someone else to take the lead in your life. You are not always questioning when you don't see the manifestation in your time. You believe in each other. And *temperance* means to display self-control. The more and more we try to get away from it we can't; we need to be discipline. We need to be able to control our feelings (emotions).

The Bible tells us that it's okay to be angry just don't sin *(Ephesians 4:26)*. The only way to release the anger we may feel from time to time without going into a rage and sin against God and man is to have control over our mind and emotions. God wants to give us the desires of His heart. If you want a spouse then ask, and prepare for it. When Esther got married, her purpose was to stop the Jews from being destroyed. God told me that there are people waiting on me to deliver them. And there are people waiting on me and my spouse to link up. God is a God of timing and if it's your time embrace it and stop allowing people to change what God has already told you. God is a God of preparation so get up, get ready, and get moving. Start allowing God to change your vision and align your desire up with His. He knows what you need in order to prosper in this life because He planned it out. Your spouse must accommodate every part of your future. God knows what He's doing and He won't fail you. So I challenge you to let Him lay the right foundation and build you in His image so that you can be ready. If you stay in your process and discipline your mind, body, soul, and spirit you will be ready for your King or Queen!!!

## Q&A

How important is it to produce a harvest?

What are some things you like to produce together as couples?

Are you connected to the one that will bring in your harvest?

Note taking below!

# Love Letters

## Letter to the men

If we journey throughout history we will find that God always used men when it came down to leading a nation and changing some form of system. Yes! He used women but let's face it the majority of people He called were men. As hard as it is to admit it I now realize that men are better when it comes to leading nations. Why? Because Men have a natural intellect to lead. The enemy wants to destroy Gods divine order by destroying the identity of our men and by rearranging the alignment of heaven. You will find that men hold their composure in the mist of adversity a little better. They were created to hold their emotional and mental capacity together. Two things will hinder his ability to lead, and that's pride and fear. Both areas attack their intellect but fear will always affect your emotions. Once the mind has become infected with pride and fear then he no longer has the ability to lead because leading is an unselfish act. The difference between David and Saul was that Saul's intellect was infected with pride and fear that spread to his emotions.

Now let me stop and say that men do have emotions but for some reason they can control it better then women. Men who become emotional lose their ability to lead nations because the enemy comes in while they are babes. His main goal is to create an imbalance in their mind and emotions. There are many emotional men that are great leaders. Because they didn't allow their emotions to destroy them. Greatness was destined to happen. Some emotional men will feel the suppressing of their purpose to lead, and will lead in their own opinion of things. The unselfish act to lead becomes a selfish attempt to get others to succumb to his way of thinking. Although their minds have become infected with pride and fear it is brought on by an underlying condition called deception. Deception is what I like to call an autoimmune disease.

The immune system is a system of biological structures and processes within an organism that protects against diseases. When the immune system becomes infected it loses its ability to function and cannot fight off other diseases leaving them open for attack. Deception shuts down your ability to think and receive. You become opinionated. That's when pride begins to take root and slowly kills you. Men cannot afford to be led by their emotions. They were created to be strong, supportive of women, and carry nations. Men can only retain their ability to lead in their mind and vision. Spiritual and naturally growth is found in the mind. Not Sexuality! Men must never rush the process because it's creating a balance in their manhood. When God created men, He created them to be visionaries. Not only do they see with their eyes but they think with their eyes. In the book of Genesis God instructed Adam to name each living creature?

*Genesis 2:19 Out of the ground the Lord God formed every beast of the field and every bird of the air, and brought them to Adam to see what he would call them. And whatever Adam called each living creature that was its name.*

Adam was given the ability to see what heaven called each animal in order to speak effectively into their lives. When God created Eve, He took her to Adam. When Adam saw her, he declared that she shall be called the woman because she was taken out of him. Adam was even given the privilege to name her. So why did God create Eve? When God instructed Adam to name the animals, he looked around and didn't see anyone that would suit him. My question is what was he basing it on? The animals! What would have happened, if he would've chosen from among the animals? The reason Eve was taken out of man was because Adam needed someone to help him carry out the future plans of God. He couldn't choose based upon what he saw from his past. He saw someone who resembled his abilities. Someone, he could become one with.

*Genesis 2:24 Therefore shall a man leave his father and mother and be joined to his wife, and they shall become one flesh.*

Man and woman were created to complete one another mentally, spiritually, physically, emotionally, and financially. Being one requires us to be whole and not divided. The first thing that the enemy will attack with a man is his vision. Perception is a matter of the mind. It creates visual images in your head to influence your thinking. The enemy knows that man's authority is tied to his ability to see. They must be able to see into God's eternal kingdom if they are going to speak effectively into the earth.

## *Letter to the women*

As women, we must understand the nature of our men as it relates to their manhood. The only reason men feel the need to give up is because their manhood has been attacked. When they feel like they can't provide for themselves and others, it causes them to succumb to the spirit of anger. We have a huge social and economic crisis due to poverty. Men are fighting to support their families and it causes them to steal, kill, and sell illegal substances. Not because he's an animal but because he's fighting to be accepted and prove that he is a man. Young men whose Households are absent of father's natural instinct to lead kicks in and they begin engaging in criminal activity. Instead of developing the character traits of a man they develop flaws that not only define his character but a whole race of people. It is very important that women understand how to build up their house.

The bible says that a wise woman builds up her house but a foolish woman tares it down. We have to understand them and encourage them to be all that God has created them to be giving the enemy no room. Statements like a real man makes his own fortune has a negative impact on them. When men become ill, are laid off, or find it hard to make ends meet their manhood is attacked daily. In their minds, they have to live up to the standards of society, church, and their families. My desire for women is that we see men not for what they are supposed to do for us, but what we are supposed to do for each other. When we learn to value them as leaders and the head of your household then you are ready to meet your king!

## *LOVE Letter*

Love is an expression of how we feel, and our feelings have the power to change depending upon the moment. Love requires no immediate action. It's a knowing that their presence or the aroma of it is there. We love God and we don't see Him. Even though He's not there, the love and relationship we build with Him allow us to feel Him when He's not there. Even the expectation of God working behind the stage move's us into a state of gratefulness. When times are hard, we take a stand by standing on what He has promised us. A man whom we've never seen, we believe he loved us based on the cross. We often declare Lord if you never do anything else, you've already done enough. It's the same way with man and woman. Even when we don't see the love through our actions, we must have a knowing. We must feel and smell the aroma of their presence when they leave the room. Love is not a feeling we encounter for a moment, but a scent that lingers. It's ok to enjoy the moment, but never allow yourself to live for the moment. Moments are design to change. Love is not based on the length of time we've spent with each other. It's based on the acceptance of our needs, wants, flaws, and desires. Love helps us to accept our differences and teaches us the art of compromise.

Without acceptance intimacy will only bear bad fruit. The enemy-tainted Adam and Eve level of intimacy.

Love is long suffering. It's respecting and accepting others, its reliability and accountability, its truth and trustworthy. It's pushing each other forward and refusing to leave others behind, its compassion, and patience. It's empowering and being real. It's fighting and praying for each other. It's building and extorting others. It's being there in hard times and great times. It's communicating and listening. It's accepting, losing, and winning sometimes. It's understanding who we are and not forcing change, but empowering change. It's sacrificing for the better. It's dying to oneself to produce as partners. It's knowing your part and perfecting it. It's caring and taking care of others. It's responding and knowing how to respond. It's sharing the spot in being first. It's feeding so we can grow and live. It's thinking before you speak. It's relational, getting to know others. It's learning something new and throwing out the old. It's forgiving so you can be forgiven. It believes when no one else believes. It's being there in hard times to comfort. It's remembering the purpose and working together to fulfill it. It's following and obeying what's right. Love cost and is priceless. It protects and covers. It's warm and sweet. It's an experience we all were created to have. It forms our character and creates our inner circle. It's how we influence the world and change it. It calms us, and refreshes us. It's how we birth things in the earth realm. It stops crimes, and heals broken hearts. It sees ahead. It teaches our children how to become leaders. It changes as it grows. It will bring us to our knees and it's how the world is being sustained. Love covers all things and all sins. It will never fail!

**Never fail!**

# List of love not

- *Loves not puffed up*
- *Loves not silent*
- *Love don't kill*
- *Love don't reject*
- *Love don't lie*
- *Love don't condemn*
- *Love never stop growing*
- *Love never separate*
- *Love isn't intimidated by other emotions*
- *Love isn't being blind*
- *Love don't expose your weakness publicly*
- *Love don't seek its own*
- *Love don't disrespect you*

There is a lot we can say about love when it comes to building relationships. Love is the most powerful tool to use in this world. God loved us so much that He sent His son to save us. If you want to build effective relationships, you must first learn to love yourself and others. People follow those they trust and they trust those they believe love them and want the best for them. When people love you become empowered. Love is the only emotion that carries a scent when you're not around. Love plants a seed that grows in the heart and mind. If you want people to follow, leave your scent behind. The goal is to heal. Love covers your flaws and won't allow them to be exposed in a place that will wound you.

## *Truth*

What can we say about truth? Well, love must precede truth and truth isn't established without love. So relationships are better sustained when we learn to love one another with truth. Which mean it should be built on truth. No lies! Everyone makes mistakes but taking ownership of the truth is what keeps lasting relationships growing. The reason we don't tell the truth when we connect to people is because we don't trust. It is impossible to go through life not trusting because life is about connecting to people and helping them accomplish their goals in life. The Bible says you shall know the truth and only the truth can set you free. Leaders take responsibility and ownership of the vision. If you cannot trust or tell your team the truth when it fails it will be because of you. Truth helps me understand you. It helps me to love you in spite of your weaknesses. When truth is present there is no need to establish proof. There is no second guessing. It's like the building of a house. It sustains the relationship because it's the foundation of it. The enemy doesn't like relationships. So he sows discord.

He takes the foundation of the truth and starts to build upon it. The only way to know if the foundation of your relationship is founded on truth is when an attack comes or a storm. The storm might destroy the house but as long as the foundation is intact you can rebuild. Relationships are about learning from each other not belittling each other. If we don't allow ourselves to open up and tell the truth how can you embrace your help? Truth means admitting your failures. It means admitting you are not as great as you think you are. Truth always exposes the length of time we've spent with each. It helps me to be true to myself and others. I can freely love when truth is there. I can empower when truth is there. I can lead when truth is there I can trust when truth is there, and I can have victory when truth is there.

# Advice Column (: Michael Franklin)

- Why do men have a problem communicating their weakness to women? (Michael) Because he feels, he can't trust her, and he doesn't want to give her things to use against him.

- Why is it hard to let go of a woman when you know she's not the one? (Michael) It's hard to start over, and that person has become family to you. Also, you may have ties to her.

- How important is hygiene? Is it something a relationship can recover from? (Michael) It's no relationship if her body doesn't smell right, and it would be impossible to recover from. Her scent is one of the things that will draw us.

- When a man has been wounded by a woman, what are some of the mental attacks he goes through? (Michael) He begins to battle in his mind with a thought about her telling his secrets and he's afraid she might tell people.

- Is there anything a woman can do to bring healing to a man when he's been wounded from a past relationship? (Michael) Yes, she can do things he always wanted, and her ability to trust, communicate, and be good in the bedroom makes him feel appreciated.

- What can women do to help a man when his manhood has been challenged? (Michael) Never disrespect his size and encourage him to continue to build for his future.

- What's the most important thing men look for in a woman? (Michael) He actually looks for her ability to lead. Although we have to take charge and lead. Men like to know that their woman can hold things down without them.

- What defines a woman? (Michael) A woman who knows her worth. A woman who's not threatened by other women when it comes to understanding her man etc. A women who takes charge, and control of her mind, body, soul, and spirit. No crybabies!

- What are the expectations a lot of men put on women? (Michael) Some may expect her to be equal to them when it comes to finances /work, and being responsible for the whole house, and the kids.

- Do you believe a marriage can recover from infidelity? (Michael) Yes, there are a lot of men that can forgive, but there must be a healing process.

- Does trauma from a man's past determine how he treats women? (Michael) Yes, his past will define his manhood and his ability to lead his family. So deliverance is always required to grow. Our past will cause us to shut down and become fearful. Wounds from our past sometimes lead us to feel threaten by thinking she wants to control him. Which is why we don't want to express our emotions.

- What changes are necessary to help you adjust to each other's future? (Michael) Considering our family, finances, vision, and how we need to proceed forward.

## *Quotes*

- When you are connected to a person long enough their action and their speech will let you know if you will be free to expose parts of you.

- Our perception of others is based on self-freedom. If we don't submit to a process of inner-healing we will continue to see others through flawed lenses.

- I told myself, if I don't allow God to heal me, I would end up marrying someone who reflects my past, or someone who I thought was suitable for my present. Meanwhile, I risk losing the one who could accommodate my future.

- The love I have for you will only allow me to stand with you in truth. It doesn't cover someone who has taken comfort in a lie. I have the power to love you through your flaws but you have to trust me enough to be honest about them. Your relationship should be founded on truth.

- When a man tells you, "let's be friends and see where it leads", he gives the relationship hope and direction. He knows that hope and direction are the fuel that keeps a woman holding on.

- There were times I stayed committed to his word even when he did keep his word.

- There are a lot of men who have missed their good thang because they couldn't see themselves with a woman with children. Joseph is the definition of a real man. He was chosen to raise the Messiah because he was willing to take care of someone else's responsibility. Remember your marriage is going to have an assignment. Question is are you willing to submit to it.

## Toxic relationships

- Leave you feeling drained
- Leave you feeling trapped, leave you feeling empty
- Leave you feeling worthless
- Leave you questioning your manhood/womanhood
  Leave you feeling you're the problem just to draw attention away from them
- When a toxin has infected a relationship, it will cause a shortage and stop your growth and development. Defeating the purpose of two becoming one.

- If the foundation of your relationship is stable, you will be able to withstand the storms. Which will help you to keep building? This will generate unwavering faith and give you longevity.

**Tools for personal development**

Personal development is about improvement and discovering one's true identity. It's developing new gifts and unlocking hidden talents.

- **_Self-aware_**- *being aware of what makes you different and unique.*

- **_Self-knowledge_**- *researching your gifts and callings. Invest your time and energy and resources into it. Never give all your time to people. You must invest your mind in you.*

- **_Self-leader_**- *learning to lead you before leading others. Take yourself down a path of personal success.*

- **_Self-empowerment_**- *empower yourself to make good sound decisions for your present and future.*

- **_Self- discipline_**- *not being afraid of sacrificing for yourself. You must value you and bring enrichment to self.*

## Principles

- *Have people skills*

- *Get inner healing*

- *Create a positive thought pattern*

- *Learn the art of listening*

- *Learn to communicate*

### *Communications, shutting down and pretending!*

Communication is very important in every relationship involving God and man. It's one of the main components. Although there are many ways to communicate with each other there are only five major areas in which I will list:

- *Body language*
- *Written*
- *How we say things*
- *Facial expressions*
- *Words we speak*

It's important to know that our body postures can make us feel loved, appreciated, used, and abused. Every time something happens in my life it caused me to shut down. I would stop communicating with people on a personal level. I would talk but not let them into my life. In the beginning of 2013, I was told that this was my season for marriage. During my process, God informed me that I had to stop shutting down on people when I get mad. He said that it would affect my marriage. I begin to seek advice from women whose marriage ended in divorce. I found out that many couples had a hard time communicating because one spouse would shut down on them, or wouldn't open up at all. It was due to open wombs not being healed before the marriage. This was a huge problem for me. But never the less I'm over it. When I study what it meant to shut something down I was blown away, it means it has come to an end. It has been terminated or has ceased from a way of doing things. Now I realize the dangers of it. It is not good to stop talking to anyone or not deal with your problems. Whether it's a friend, family, husband, or wife. God wants us to be able to deal with confrontation. When you are in a partnership and a disagreement arise; you unplug your mind and ear from the problem what happens? You won't hear so you can't understand, and you can't hear from God to receive the answer to the solution.

Shutting down means both partners can't come to an agreement. Now I know we all say we hate politics but let's think about how the government shutting down impacted this nation. Because all parties couldn't come to an agreement funds were withheld. Hint! Do you really think God is going to release your wealth if you are not in agreement? Just like other services were shut down due to their discussion. It's the same way in a partnership. Our commitment levels to the things we are managing begin to fail, and as a result, the kids are affected. That's why it's important to deal with the spirit before getting into any partnership. Sometimes shutting down on someone will cause you to pretend. I was so good at pretending that everything was alright. Even going as far as showering them with gifts. Gifts were and still are the best way to pretend you care about someone. When you pretend that you have forgiven someone you hold up your blessing. God won't release what you want if you are holding on to unforgiveness. There are a lot of things God had to clean out of me, and that was one. Now I can enter my marriage free and clear and wait to receive our increase.

*Romans 12:9*

***Don't just pretend to love others. Really love them. Hate is wrong. Hold tightly to what is good. Love each other with genuine affections, and take delight in honoring each other.***

The key to a healthy partnership is to stay connected to the source of the partnership (God). Love each other with a genuine heart accepting flaws and all. Allow God to heal all open wombs, and every scar that will hinder you from producing a harvest.

## *Q&A!*

- How long have you been single?
- What are the things you are willing to compromise?
- Are you ready to share?
- What are the hidden pains from your past?
- What has God said concerning your spouse?
- Are you commitment to God?
- Are you angry?
- Has your mind been renewed?
- What are the areas that need work?

- Are you ready for discipline?
- How well do you flow with others?
- How large is your capacity to handle things?
- What are your expectations about your marriage? Are you carnal minded?

## *Ten things to remember!*

- Stay connected in the spirit
- Your flesh is connected to the idea of you being together sexually
- Your marriage is a ministry but you both have been given an assignment.
- There are instructions that God will give you to follow as a couple.
- Know and remain faithful to the covenant with God and each other
- If you are not willing to compromise your standards before the marriage how well will you be able to compromise in the marriage. (Something's need to be compromised. But make sure it's from the Lord)
- Compromise is a mutual agreement
- Value each other's differences.
- Communication is the foundations, and listening is the key to understanding each other's present desires.
- Keep learning from each other.

### Scriptures and prayers!

*1 Corinthians 9: 27*

*I discipline my body like an athlete, training it to do what it should. Otherwise, I fear that after preaching to others I be disqualified.*

Father, I pray that you will release a greater flow of discipline in my life as well as my spouse. I pray that we will stay focus on our assignment. I pray against the spirit of procrastination. We will be overcomers in Jesus name Amen!

## Ecclesiastes 4:9-12

*It is better to have a partner than to go at it alone. Share the work. Share the wealth and if one fall down the other help, but if there is no one to help, tough! Two in a bed warm each other. Alone you shiver all night. By yourself you've unprotected. With a friend, you can face the worst. Can you round up a third? A three-stranded rope isn't easily snapped.*

Father, I thank you for thinking about me. Father, you saw my need and answered my prayer. You said in your word that two is better than one. I declare in the name of Jesus Christ that we will enjoy our process we will enjoy our journey. I declare and decree we will work together. We will share every assignment. We will learn from each other, and we will protect one another. I decree that if one falls down we will be there to catch each other. Father, we will be willing to face whatever comes our way in Jesus name **Amen!**

## Psalms 37:5

*Commit thy way unto the Lord; trust also in him and he shall bring it to pass.*

Father, I repent right now for not trusting you with my whole heart. I repent for not expecting greater from you because you are great. Teach me oh Lord how to be faithful and committed because I know that you are able to bring it to pass.

## 1 Corinthians 3:9

*For we are all God's follow worker. You are God's field, God's building.* Lord, I pray that you will remove everything out of me that's unclean. Build me, mold me, and reshape me back into your image. Restore my character of you Lord and make me more like you. I belong to you. You created me and you will sustain me in Jesus name.

## 1 Corinthians 3:11

*Remember there is one foundation, the one already laid. Jesus Christ! Take particular care in picking out your building materials. Eventually, there is going to be an inspection.*

Lord, I thank you for laying a righteous foundation within me. Everything you have created is perfect. Lord continue to prepare me to be inspected in my due season. I come against the spirit of fear, against every mind controlling demon that will try and hinder me from believing in myself. I will be ready for my spouse in my season. I will wait on God and will stay in my process. I can do all things because the foundation of Christ lives within me Amen!

## Isaiah 9:3

*You have multiplied the nation; you have increased its joy; they rejoice before you as with joy at the harvest, as they are glad when they divide the spoil.*

Thank you Daddy God for you have increased the fruit of my labor. You've caused my cup to run over. For I have received an increase in my singleness. Lord, I will trust you forever more. I thank you even now for the increase in my marriage while being still in my singleness. I pray my marriage will be filled with joy and peace, and increase in wealth in Jesus name Amen!

Father protects my spouse from sickness and disease. I pray that no weapon formed against him will be able to prosper. I pray against the spirit of perversions, the spirit of homosexually, and abuse. I pray that you will connect us in the spirit; I pray that we will heed your voice. Father, I pray that we will wait on you. I pray that we will be a man and woman of integrity, wisdom and virtue. Father God move upon our lives like never before. Refresh, renew, and make us more like you. I pray that every inner vow will be broken; every form of UN-forgiveness will be uprooted from our heart. I pray that we will walk in the fruits of the spirit. I pray that we will be committed to our love for each other, and committed to the covenant(s) we make to you. I declare that we will take our mountain; we will hear and allow you to lead us. I declare that we will be empowered with your love and peace; we will take the land and be an example of you. Father God decrease us and increase us with more of you. I pray against the spirit of witchcraft and every demonic spirit that's trying to stop this relationship, every generational curse, and every negative word that was, is, and will be spoken over our life's we break it now I declare and decree that it's done in Jesus name Amen!

## Understanding his and her needs Journal

# References

**King James/Spirit Filled Thomas Nelson 2002**

J. Choquel. (2013-2014). The 4 different stages of sleep (NREM

    Stages 1, 2 and 3, plus REM sleep).  Retrieved from

    http://blog.withings.com/2015/03/17/the-4-different-
    stages-of-sleep/

In *Merriam - Webster Dictionary*. Retrieved from

    http://www.merriam-webster.com/

99441037R00050

Made in the USA
Lexington, KY
19 September 2018